AMAZING HOCKEY STORIES

P.K. SUBBAN

Lorna Schultz Nicholson
Illustrations by D. A. Bishop

Scholastic Canada Ltd.
Toronto New York London Auckland Sydney
Mexico City New Delhi Hong Kong Buenos Aires

Scholastic Canada Ltd.
604 King Street West, Toronto, Ontario M5V 1E1, Canada

Scholastic Inc.
557 Broadway, New York, NY 10012, USA

Scholastic Australia Pty Limited
PO Box 579, Gosford, NSW 2250, Australia

Scholastic New Zealand Limited
Private Bag 94407, Botany, Manukau 2163, New Zealand

Scholastic Children's Books
Euston House, 24 Eversholt Street, London NW1 1DB, UK

www.scholastic.ca

Library and Archives Canada Cataloguing in Publication

Schultz Nicholson, Lorna, author
P.K. Subban / Lorna Schultz Nicholson ; illustrated by D.A. Bishop.

(Amazing hockey stories)
ISBN 978-1-4431-7024-6 (softcover)

1. Subban, P. K., 1989- --Juvenile literature. 2. Hockey players--
Canada--Biography--Juvenile literature. I. Title. II. Series: Schultz
Nicholson, Lorna. Amazing hockey stories.

GV848.5.S92S39 2019   j796.962092   C2018-906659-8

Photos ©: cover: Danny Murphy/Icon Sportswire/Getty Images; 5: John Russell/
NHLI/Getty Images; 8: Dave Sandford/NHLI/Getty Images; 10: Brian Babineau/
NHLI/Getty Images; 17: Claus Andersen/Getty Images; 22: Dave Sandford/Getty
Images; 24: Sean Kilpatrick/Canadian Press Images; 31: Adrian Wyld/Canadian
Press Images; 33: Boris Minkevich/Canadian Press Images; 35: Len Redkoles/
NHLI/Getty Images; 37: Jamie Sabau/Getty Images; 38: Lauren Peterson/AHL;
44: Francois Lacasse/NHLI/Getty Images; 45: Tasos Katopodis/Getty Images;
47: Bruce Bennett/Getty Images; 49: Graham Hughes/Canadian Press Images;
51: John Russell/NHLI/Getty Images; 60: John Russell/NHLI/Getty Images; 62:
John Russell/NHLI/Getty Images; 64: Eliot J. Schechter/NHLI/Getty Images.

6 5 4 3 2 1   Printed in Malaysia 108   19 20 21 22 23

CONTENTS

LARGER THAN LIFE

Everyone knows the hard-hitting, big-grinning Nashville Predators defenceman as P.K. Subban, but his full name is Pernell Karl Sylvester Subban. Even during his earliest years in hockey, people talked about P.K. "Who is that kid who can skate like that . . . and shoot like that?" they would ask. His slapshot made players on the opposing team cringe and often move out of the way. And sometimes P.K. stood out for more than his skills. At that time there weren't very many players who were visible minorities. But that never stopped him from working as hard as he could to achieve his goals.

P.K. has always been a standout off the ice as well as on it. He is known for his generosity — P.K.'s support of children's charities is legendary. And he's got a magnetic, larger-than-life personality. Whenever he's near a microphone or a camera, he owns the show — his quick wit has made him a media favourite. You can tell P.K. really enjoys being P.K.!

Today, in his NHL career, P.K. still has his famous bullet shot, but he has worked hard on every aspect of his game. His skating and stickhandling skills allow him to weave through traffic to get to the net. And score goals. He knocks opponents out of his way like bowling pins, shoots like a rocket and skates like a charging bull every second he is on the ice.

Whatever P.K. Subban does, he does with fierce determination and passion. And probably a huge smile.

P.K. IS KNOWN FOR HIS SLAPSHOT. IT HAS BEEN CLOCKED AT 164.6 KM/H (102.3 MPH).

P.K.

P.K. was born on May 13, 1989, in Toronto, Ontario. He is the oldest boy and middle child in a family of five kids. P.K.'s mother, Maria, came to Canada from the Caribbean island of Montserrat in 1970, the same year that his father, Karl, moved from Jamaica to Sudbury, Ontario. Before P.K., they had his two older sisters, Nastassia and Natasha. Then they had Pernell Karl, who added a different dynamic to the family. P.K. was so full of energy! A few years later, two younger brothers, Malcolm and Jordan, came along. Like their big brother, they are both terrific hockey players.

MIDNIGHT SKATES

The Subban family were big hockey fans. From the time P.K.'s dad arrived in Canada, he loved *Hockey Night in Canada*, and he watched it faithfully. He had a dream that his children would learn to skate like other Canadian kids. P.K. was just two years old when he started skating — on a pair of his sister's hand-me-down figure skates! He quickly caught on and graduated to his first pair of hockey skates . . .

and then learned to skate in earnest. By the time he was three, P.K. and his dad were hitting the public rinks. P.K.'s dad believed that skating was vitally important to being a good hockey player. By age four, P.K. could zip around the other skaters.

When P.K. was five, he skated almost every day, including at Toronto City Hall, which was the first outdoor rink in the city to freeze. In those days, P.K.'s dad worked in the evenings and P.K.'s mom was busy with the family. P.K. would go to bed dressed in his snowsuit, and his dad would wake him up at 10:00 p.m. and drive him downtown to City Hall. Little P.K. would play shinny with the adults, sometimes until well after midnight! Sometimes he begged his father to "stay longer." His kindergarten class was in the afternoon, so he got to sleep in the next day. Once the rinks in Etobicoke opened for public skating, P.K. could skate a bit closer to home. The Subban family also built a backyard rink so P.K. and his siblings could skate all the time.

WHAT ARE P.K.'S NICKNAMES?

SUBBANATOR, SUBBY AND SUBBZ.

P.K. HAS SPENT HIS WHOLE LIFE WORKING HARD ON HIS SKATING, WHICH HE SHOWS OFF HERE AT THE 2016 NHL ALL-STAR SKILLS COMPETITION.

TIME FOR A TEAM

P.K. was just four years old when he joined his first organized hockey team, the Flames, which were part of the house league program at Chris Tonks Arena in Toronto. Because P.K. was such a strong skater, he was put on a team with players who were two and three years older than he was! But it didn't take P.K. long to adjust to team play.

The following year, P.K. joined the house league program at Pine Point Arena in Etobicoke. Even though he had just turned five in May, he also played on an all-star team made up of six-year-olds. But P.K. wasn't intimidated — he was big for his age and could play hard. The all-star team was made up of the best kids from the house league program and they played extra games during the season. That year P.K. scored 19 of the team's 21 goals. Everyone was buzzing about the talented young player.

P.K. was soon ready for more. The following season he joined a select team, the West Mall Lightning Super 8s in Etobicoke. They were called the Super 8s because that's how old the other players were. P.K. was only six years old and was so good that no one knew the difference.

By the time he was nine, P.K. was playing novice hockey for the North York Junior Canadiens of the GTHL (Greater Toronto Hockey League). P.K. wasn't the only future NHLer on that team, either — Steven Stamkos and Chris Tanev were on it, too! It was an exciting year for P.K. The Junior Canadiens had the best regular-season record in their division *and* they won the Toronto championship.

WHO IS P.K.'S FAVOURITE PLAYER?

BOBBY ORR!

P.K. AND STEVEN STAMKOS HAVE BEEN GOOD
FRIENDS SINCE PLAYING TOGETHER IN THE GTHL.

In April 1999, P.K. was recruited by the Toronto Red Wings, a minor atom AAA team in the Greater Toronto Hockey League. He played summer hockey with them until July. When the team took a break for summer vacation, he kept on training. P.K. attended the PASS hockey school run by Kam Brothers, as he did many summers. He was ready to go when the Red Wings started up again in early September, and the season ahead looked great after they won their first early bird tournament.

But then things seemed to quickly go downhill for P.K. and the Red Wings.

A BIGGER STAGE

P.K. had his fair share of ups and downs as he worked through the ranks of minor hockey. Some of his teams didn't win a lot of games. Learning how to lose wasn't always easy, but P.K. kept an upbeat attitude. If they couldn't win, at least the team could rely on P.K. to make a play, so he concentrated on his game. Sometimes people taunted him for the colour of his skin. P.K. ignored them. And he also ignored the coaches and some of the other players' parents who told him that he'd never make it in hockey. The best way to win was on the ice, so he focused on that. He was determined to achieve his dream: playing in the NHL.

LOOK OUT BELLEVILLE, HERE COMES A BULL

A week before P.K. turned 16, he sat in front of a computer to watch the names being chosen for the Ontario Hockey League Priority Selection draft. First round. Second round. Third round. More and more names. Fourth round. Finally, in the sixth round, P.K. was drafted by the Belleville Bulls.

The percentage of players who actually play in the OHL after being drafted past the fourth round is small. P.K. wondered if his dream of playing in the NHL was even possible. Then George Burnett, P.K.'s new coach, phoned him to welcome him personally to the Bulls. This small gesture inspired P.K. and gave him the fuel he needed to train hard all summer.

To get ready for the OHL training camp, P.K. travelled an hour from Toronto to Cambridge at least four times a week — sometimes twice a day! — to work with a coach who trained many OHL players. They did drills on the track and weights in the gym, as well as ice sessions with other junior and pro players.

When he hit the ice for Belleville's training camp he was ready. It was intense, but the Bulls liked what they saw in the determined 16-year-old. Coach Burnett said, "It was special that we were able to find a player in the sixth round who turned out to be of his talent . . . he brought such a terrific attitude and work ethic and set of skills to the rink each and every day."

At the end of camp, including pre-season games, P.K. was signed for the 2005–06 season. He was going to be a Belleville Bull after all.

P.K. BECAME A STAR FOR THE BELLEVILLE BULLS. AS A SIXTH-ROUND PICK, HE WAS CONSIDERED A "STEAL" FOR THE TEAM.

At the time, the Belleville Yardmen Arena had an Olympic-sized rink, which is four metres wider than a standard NHL rink. P.K. quickly learned how to use the extra space to his advantage. He would rush up the ice, barrel through opponents and make risky, daring plays. P.K. loved to have the puck on the end of his stick, to control the play. He'd pick up the puck, skate like the wind, sometimes lose the puck, but then get it back so he could take a shot on net . . . or maybe lose it again. Or maybe wipe out. Or make an assist on a goal. Every shift was exciting when P.K. was on the ice.

When reporters questioned George Burnett about "reining in his hotshot," he said, "That's just P.K. being P.K." The fans in Belleville loved him for his high-speed rushes, gutsy moves, and for his energy. P.K. was better entertainment than television! It didn't take long for P.K. Subban to become a household name in the small city of Belleville. He became a media favourite because he always had something witty to say when he was in front of a camera. And P.K. *loved* being in front of a camera.

In his OHL rookie season in 2005–06, P.K. played 52 games and got 5 goals and 7 assists for a total of 12 points. The Bulls managed 72 points that year and made it into the playoffs. They battled the Brampton Battalion in the first round, which went to six games. Ultimately the Battalion defeated the

Bulls, but the young rookie P.K. played in three of the games, getting a taste of OHL playoff action.

In his second year with the Bulls, P.K. played in all 68 games, scoring 15 goals and a whopping 41 assists for 56 points. When it came time for the 2006–07 season playoffs, he couldn't wait to prove himself.

PLAYOFFS AND POWER PLAYS

The Bulls took charge in the first round and were soon up three games to one on the Ottawa 67's. In the fifth game of this series, P.K. popped a power-play goal in the net, helping his team to a 3–3 tie at the end of regular play. Belleville won the game in overtime, and for the first time in his junior career, P.K. was moving on to the second round of playoffs.

Round two saw the Bulls sweep the Oshawa Generals in just four games. In game two, P.K. assisted on a power-play goal in the first period and scored back-to-back goals in the second period to help Belleville win 5–2. P.K. earned his first big playoff accolade and was named first star of the game. Two wins later the Bulls were off to the conference final against the Sudbury Wolves.

This series was a battle, with three of the first five games going into OT. Sudbury was up 3–2 heading into game six, so the Bulls *had* to win this one. The lead went back and forth, and at the final buzzer the teams were tied 3–3. They were headed into an overtime period. And then a second one. And then a third! The players desperately wanted the win, and they were tired — a time when it's easy to make a mistake. At 2:56 into the third overtime period, the whistle blew — it was an interference call against P.K. He skated to the penalty box, unable to help his team during the Wolves power play. The seconds ticked by. Sudbury hammered away. Then at 3:23, they put the puck past the Bulls goalie. P.K.'s penalty had cost his team the game.

It was a hard moment. But as Coach Burnett put it, "P.K. doesn't have too many bad days and when he does, it's hard to tell." P.K. knew he had helped the Bulls make it to the playoffs twice now, and this time he had scored five goals and earned eight assists. But over the summer, P.K. hit his training regimen harder than ever. Overtime or not, he knew he could improve.

TIME FOR THE SHOW?

On June 22, 2007, at the NHL Entry Draft, P.K. Subban waited in the stands at Nationwide Arena in Columbus, Ohio, wearing a stylish suit from his favourite Toronto tailor. He was so nervous that his stomach churned. The first round was called, and those players made their way to the stage. P.K. wasn't one of them. Then in the second round, in the 43rd spot, his name was called by the Montreal Canadiens! It didn't matter to P.K. that 16 other defencemen had been called before him. Numbers and stats didn't scare him one bit. P.K. just wanted a chance to prove himself.

P.K. was especially happy to be drafted by Montreal. Back when he was a kid, playing hockey for the Mississauga Reps, a special guest stopped by the team's dressing room to give the team a pre-game talk. It was Jean Beliveau, who had played 20 seasons with the Montreal Canadiens! P.K. hung on every word he said. Beliveau even talked to P.K. personally and told him that as the team captain he always had to play for his team first. P.K. had never forgotten the advice . . . and now he had the chance to *be* a Montreal Canadien!

EVEN THOUGH P.K. GREW UP IN TORONTO, HE ALWAYS LOVED CHEERING FOR THE MONTREAL CANADIENS.

The Canadiens selected P.K. because of what they saw both on and off the ice. They said that P.K. "can be a bit of a pest to play against" and that he also "has a real hard point shot. Physically he's powerful and he's in great shape." They recognized P.K.'s larger-than-life personality, too, saying, "He's soon going to be a favourite among the beat scribes [reporters] in Montreal. He's full of energy and that's what makes him, him."

TEAM CANADA

The Canadiens weren't the only ones who had noticed P.K.'s talent. Just weeks after the draft, P.K. was invited to a Hockey Canada World Junior development camp. Only 45 players from across Canada had been chosen to attend the July camp in Ottawa. Eighteen-year-old P.K. was pumped. Maybe he'd get to play in the World Junior Hockey Championship in the Czech Republic at Christmastime! When it was time for the camp, P.K. suited up and played his heart out. After the development camp ended, Hockey Canada scouts would watch the players during the fall season and pick 37 players to attend a selection camp in December.

So much was happening! Like most of the second-round draft picks, P.K. wasn't going straight to the NHL, but his career was going in the right direction. It was no time to slow down. Over the summer, he trained like never before, and when he hit the ice with the Belleville Bulls in the fall of 2007, they kept winning. It was looking like they would make the playoffs for the third year in a row and maybe even finish first in the OHL's Eastern Conference. P.K. was definitely making a good impression on the Hockey Canada scouts.

In December, P.K. got the call from Hockey Canada. He'd be going to the final World Junior selection camp. But would he make the team?

ON DECEMBER 11, 2008, P.K. SUITED UP WITH 36 OTHER CONTENDERS FOR THE FIRST DAY OF TEAM CANADA TRAINING CAMP.

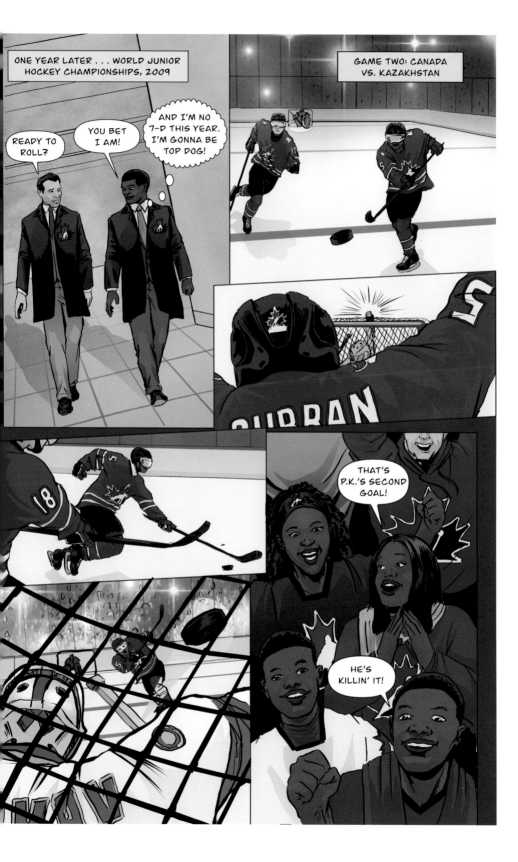

BACK IN THE BULL PEN

Determination and a positive attitude pushed P.K. through his junior hockey years. When he didn't get much ice time at the 2008 World Juniors, he didn't get discouraged. He watched and learned, and when he got back to Belleville, P.K. worked harder at practices. The Bulls were having a great year. He kept thinking: they *could* win the OHL championship. And then maybe even the Memorial Cup!

With P.K. handling the blue line, the Bulls cruised into the 2008 OHL playoffs. They barrelled through Peterborough, Barrie and Oshawa in the first three rounds, winning twelve games and losing just two. They faced the Kitchener Rangers in the finals. The championship was in reach.

The start of the series was a shocker for the Bulls and their fans — Belleville lost three straight games! In the fourth game, P.K. opened up the scoring, giving the Bulls the jump they needed to hang on, and they won in a dramatic overtime period. The Bulls carried on with a winning streak, evening up the series to make it 3–3. They had to win only one more game to capture the J. Ross Robertson Cup. But the final game was a bitter disappointment for the Bulls as they lost 4–1.

As luck would have it, though, the Kitchener Rangers were hosting the Memorial Cup. And as the runner-up in the host city's league, the Bulls would have a berth. They played hard in the round robin, opening with a win and a loss. In their final round-robin game, the Bulls faced their nemesis: the Kitchener Rangers. The first period saw the Rangers in control, with three unanswered goals. Going to the dressing room, P.K. knew his team had to do something — and *he* needed to step it up. The Bulls hung in and scored two goals in the second period, with P.K. assisting on the second one. The third period went scoreless until the last minute. With just twenty seconds left on the clock, P.K. blasted a shot in the back of the net to tie the game. This was huge! The Bulls went on to win the game and move on to the next round. But they couldn't make it last in the semifinal, losing to the dreaded Rangers 9–0.

The loss was frustrating, embarrassing and a hard way to end the season. Some critics said P.K. rushed too much as a defenceman, getting caught out of position, that he was still a defensive liability. But P.K. didn't let what people said get him down. He decided to buckle down and work on his defensive skills during the summer.

P.K. COLLIDES WITH KITCHENER RANGERS PLAYER JUSTIN AZEVEDO DURING THE MEMORIAL CUP SEMIFINAL ON MAY 23, 2008.

P.K. came back for the 2008–09 season determined to be consistent in his defensive play as well as dynamic on offence. And he proved those critics wrong. In regular-season action, P.K. played 56 games and had 14 goals and a whopping 62 assists. It was his highest points total ever with the Bulls.

Belleville was heading into the playoffs again! Having just won gold in the 2009 World Juniors, P.K. knew how good winning felt and wanted to bring it for the fans in Belleville.

The Bulls easily won the first round against the Sudbury Wolves and were to meet the Niagara Ice Dogs in the second. In game two against the IceDogs, P.K. played his heart out. He scored the game-winning overtime goal on a power play, earning first star of the game. Bellville beat Niagara 4–1 in the series and moved on again. Hopes were high. They faced the Brampton Battalion in the semifinal. In game one, P.K. scored two goals, his first unassisted. But it wasn't enough and sadly the Bulls lost that game . . . and the series. Brampton eliminated the Bulls — and P.K.'s last chance to be an OHL champion.

WHAT IS P.K.'S BIGGEST PET PEEVE?

WHEN PEOPLE GIVE UP.

MOVING UP

At the end of the season, George Burnett, the Bulls' coach and general manager, told P.K. he would be moving on — because P.K. was ready for his pro debut! P.K. met with the Montreal Canadiens. They'd been watching him and decided to sign him to a three-year entry-level contract. When September arrived, P.K. began the 2009–10 season with the Hamilton Bulldogs, Montreal's American Hockey League affiliate at that time. There was some controversy around signing the young hotshot.

P.K. GETS STEPPED ON BY MANITOBA MOOSE FORWARD GUILLAUME DESBIENS DURING FIRST-PERIOD AHL PLAYOFF ACTION ON APRIL 21, 2010.

Some critics said P.K.'s play was too offensive, even though he'd been working hard on the defensive element of his game. They said he jumped into the play too early and got beat — and that he might struggle in the big leagues.

But P.K. just let the negative comments roll off his back. He was determined to make the most of his AHL opportunity and to show he could be a defenceman and score — just like Bobby Orr. And he did. In his first season with the Hamilton Bulldogs, P.K. earned a lot of points. In 77 games, he scored 18 goals and 35 assists. He also tied for the AHL lead in the plus-minus category with +46. The Bulldogs made it through to the Western Conference finals and ultimately lost, but Hamilton's coach, Guy Boucher, was happy with P.K., saying, "That's where he used to have problems [defensively], but he doesn't really have that anymore. He has really matured in his game."

P.K. was also asked to play in the 2010 AHL All-Star Game. The Canadian All-Stars won the game against PlanetUSA. The All-Stars came from behind, scoring four goals in the third period to tie the game. When it went to a shootout, P.K. scored a big goal for the Canadian team and they won it 10–9! Whenever P.K. played, excitement followed.

BONJOUR, MONTREAL

Then, just a few weeks later, P.K. got the biggest opportunity of his life. The Montreal Canadiens had an injury in their lineup . . . and they were calling him up. P.K. was going to play his first NHL game! On February 12, 2010, in a game against the Philadelphia Flyers, he made his NHL debut and earned his first career point, an assist. P.K.'s debut had been a total success! He next played for the home crowd on February 13 — also against the Flyers — and earned his second career assist in the third period.

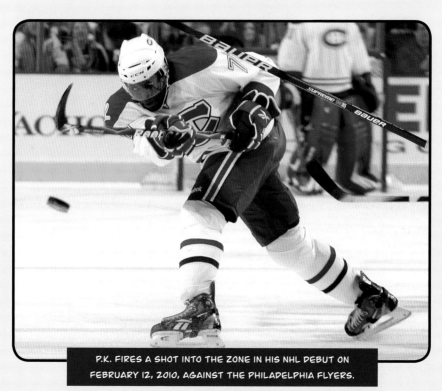

P.K. FIRES A SHOT INTO THE ZONE IN HIS NHL DEBUT ON FEBRUARY 12, 2010, AGAINST THE PHILADELPHIA FLYERS.

After the two games against the Flyers, P.K. returned to Hamilton to finish the season with the Bulldogs. The Bulldogs were heading into the AHL playoffs, and their first matchup was against the Manitoba Moose. The Bulldogs won the series 4–2, with P.K. playing in all six games. Hamilton was moving on to the North Division finals against the Abbotsford Heat.

But the Montreal Canadiens were also in the playoffs — and they wanted P.K. back on their blue line! They had another injury, and P.K. had played well for them before. On April 26, 2010, P.K. suited up in Montreal to play the Washington Capitals in his first NHL playoff game. Right from the get-go, P.K. was on fire, assisting on a goal by Mike Cammalleri. In that very first period, P.K. had earned an NHL playoff point! Montreal won the game 4–1 that night and then went on to win the series 4–3.

Next, Montreal had to play the Pittsburgh Penguins. This would be a tough series against Sidney Crosby and the team that had just won the Stanley Cup the previous season. On April 30, at 4:30 into the first period of game one, P.K. Subban recorded his first NHL goal — a blazing shot from the blue line. It was an amazing moment.

P.K. AND HIS TEAMMATES CELEBRATE HIS FIRST NHL GOAL, IN THE EASTERN CONFERENCE SEMIFINAL AGAINST THE PENGUINS ON APRIL 30, 2010.

With P.K.'s help, the Canadiens won the Eastern Conference Semifinal, beating the reigning champs in seven games. But the Canadiens' playoff run didn't last. The Philadelphia Flyers beat them in five games in the Eastern Conference Final. Still, P.K. got some big bragging rights in game three of that series, when he became just the third rookie defenceman in the team's history to earn three assists in one game. By the time their season ended, P.K. had played 14 NHL playoff games and ended up with one goal and seven assists.

To cap off P.K.'s best season yet, he was presented with the AHL's President's Award as the league's most outstanding player. This was a huge accomplishment.

P.K. had proven to his critics that he wasn't just a reckless kid. He had worked hard at being like his hero, Bobby Orr, who was offensive as well as defensive — and it had paid off. Both his AHL and NHL coaches were pleased with him.

P.K.'s dream was coming true — the Canadiens wanted him in the lineup for the upcoming season! In the fall of 2010, he was going to begin his rookie year in the NHL. P.K. was done playing in the minors.

AHL PRESIDENT DAVID ANDREWS PRESENTS P.K. WITH THE PRESIDENT'S AWARD. IT IS GIVEN IN RECOGNITION OF A PLAYER'S OUTSTANDING ACCOMPLISHMENTS FOR THAT YEAR.

BEST YEAR YET!

In his first year on the Canadiens' roster, P.K. quickly made a name for himself. Game after game, he played his heart out for the loud and boisterous crowds. He tried to learn French and he would speak it to his fans. He wasn't always good at it, but people liked that he was trying — even if they didn't always understand what he was saying.

In his first full season with the team, he played 77 games, scoring 14 goals — including his famous hat trick against Minnesota — and 24 assists for 38 points. The Canadiens made the playoffs again that year but lost to the Boston Bruins in the first round. In the 2011–12 season, P.K. played all but one game and scored 7 goals and 29 assists for 36 points. Unfortunately, the Canadiens had a tough season and didn't make the playoffs.

But 2012–13 was P.K.'s breakout year. The season was shortened to 48 games because of a labour dispute. When it finally started in January, P.K. was on fire. He played 42 of the 48 season games, scoring 11 goals and making 27 assists for 38 points — almost a point per game! P.K. earned as many points in half a season as he had in each of the last two full seasons.

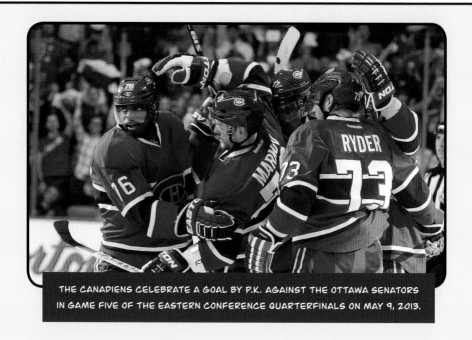

THE CANADIENS CELEBRATE A GOAL BY P.K. AGAINST THE OTTAWA SENATORS IN GAME FIVE OF THE EASTERN CONFERENCE QUARTERFINALS ON MAY 9, 2013.

He was also one of the best in the NHL on the power play, with 26 points. P.K. finished with a plus-minus of +12. This was a huge improvement over his rookie season, when he had finished with a −8. Montreal finished second in the Eastern Conference, but again didn't do very well in the playoffs and lost in the first round to Ottawa 4–1.

Although his team had been knocked out of the playoffs, P.K. got some amazing news. He was nominated for the 2013 James Norris Memorial Trophy for best defenceman in the NHL! The other finalists were Kris Letang of the Pittsburgh Penguins and Ryan Suter from the Minnesota Wild. P.K. was happy just to be nominated. He definitely didn't expect to win. The awards were given out during a television special before game two of the Stanley Cup Final. When they announced that P.K. was the winner, he was humbled — and totally thrilled!

IN 2013, P.K. WON THE JAMES NORRIS MEMORIAL TROPHY FOR BEST DEFENCEMAN IN THE NHL. WHAT AN HONOUR!

P.K. Subban improved his game every year he played in Montreal. In his 2013–14 season, P.K. scored 10 goals and 43 assists for a grand total of 53 points — and Montreal made the playoffs again.

They swept the Tampa Bay Lightning in the first round, and beat the Boston Bruins 4–3 in the second round. But then they lost the Eastern Conference Final 4–2 to the New York Rangers. The next season, P.K. earned his highest points total ever with Montreal when he finished with 60 points.

In 2014, P.K. also made the Canadian Olympic Team — and won a gold medal! Even though P.K. didn't see a lot of ice time in the Sochi Games, it was a great accomplishment to be on the team.

MONTREAL LOVES P.K.

In Montreal, P.K. Subban was so much more than his hockey game. He became someone the fans admired off the ice, too. There are so many reasons why.

P.K. enjoyed everything about Montreal, especially the fans. P.K. loved having fun with them. Sometimes he'd find a neighbourhood street hockey game and just join in, playing with the kids. Even if he was wearing sandals and jeans, he would still grab a stick and take shots on goal or run up and down passing the ball back and forth. His energy was infectious as he laughed and talked to everyone. Or at least he *tried* to talk to everyone. His French still wasn't that great.

P.K. is also a really funny guy and a bit of a prankster. He once showed up behind the scenes for a promotional television shoot dressed exactly like Don Cherry, with a wild patterned suit and tie. He imitated the famous hockey commentator so well that the show's host was doubled over laughing. During another on-air interview, P.K. joked that his brothers might be better at hockey but he was "way better looking." And he also took part in a Just For Laughs charity event in Montreal to raise money for the Montreal Children's Hospital. His jokes were so funny that the audience gave him a standing ovation!

P.K., DRESSED AS JAROMIR JAGR, LAUGHS IT UP WITH BRENT BURNS AT THE 2016 NHL ALL-STAR SKILLS COMPETITION.

But probably the biggest thing Montreal loves about P.K. Subban is his huge heart. On September 16, 2015, P.K., dressed in a sharp blue suit, entered the Montreal Children's Hospital. He was there to make a big announcement. But before he took the stage, he went around the hospital to say hi — or *bonjour* — to the young patients. Afterwards, he walked into the atrium of the hospital, where people lined three levels to see him. They were chanting his name: "P.K.! P.K.! P.K.!"

The crowd was there for the unveiling of the "Atrium P.K. Subban," named in honour of a pledge he was making to the hospital. He announced that over the next seven years his foundation would give 10 million dollars to the hospital through the P.K.'s Helping Hand charity, which assists families who have a sick child. During his speech, P.K. asked, "What do I want people to remember me for, other than being a hockey player?" Then he looked at his name on the wall and said, "Every time you walk into this hospital you'll know what I stand for."

P.K. returned to the hospital on Christmas Day with gifts for the kids. They were surprised and happy to see a real NHL player! P.K. also put out a challenge to everyone — from other players, to kids,

P.K. SPOKE TO THE CROWD IN ENGLISH AND IN FRENCH AT THE OFFICIAL OPENING OF THE P.K. SUBBAN ATRIUM / ATRIUM P.K. SUBBAN.

to the prime minister — to sing "Jingle Bells" to the children who were spending the holidays in the hospital. His challenge went viral and made a lot of sick kids very happy. Even Montrealers who weren't hockey fans loved this big-hearted player.

It was a big shock when, on June 29, 2016, it was announced that he had been traded to the Nashville Predators in exchange for fellow defenceman Shea Weber. P.K. hadn't asked for a trade. He loved his team and his city.

WHAT DID P.K. ALWAYS GET FOR CHRISTMAS?

BOOKS!

BUCKLE UP, NASHVILLE

After the trade was announced, P.K. tried to look on the bright side. In an interview he said, "I just feel good knowing a team has moved someone to bring me in because they want me. [The Nashville Predators] moved a great player, probably the last player everybody thought they would move, but they moved a great player, their captain, to bring me in and that shows a team that wants you. I'm just happy to be in a position where I can excel and feel good coming to the rink every day about myself, about the team, about my position. More importantly, I just look forward to trying to win a Stanley Cup."

Some fans and critics thought P.K. shouldn't have made the comment about the Stanley Cup. They thought he was being disrespectful to the Canadiens. He loved playing for Montreal, but he had not been able to get to the Stanley Cup Final with the Canadiens. P.K. was being honest. What player doesn't want to win the Stanley Cup?

Nashville — or "Smashville" to the fans! — didn't know what was about to hit it. When P.K. arrived in town, he headed to a legendary country music place. Wearing his trademark wide-brimmed fedora, he got up on stage and sang. There were people who said he was terrible; others said he totally nailed it, but everyone was entertained. He soon grabbed the spotlight on the ice as well. When the Predators played on October 14, 2016, it was number 76 — P.K. Subban — who scored the Predators' first goal of the season in his Nashville debut. The Predators won the game, too, beating the Chicago Blackhawks 3–2.

P.K. CELEBRATES HIS FIRST GOAL FOR THE PREDATORS WITH HIS USUAL FLAIR.

As P.K.'s first season with the Predators got underway, his remarks about making the Stanley Cup Final seemed far-fetched. In mid-December he had an upper body injury and was out for 16 games, including the first scheduled game against the Canadiens. Without P.K., the Predators still won games, but they had no consistent streaks. And when P.K. returned to the Predators' lineup, he wasn't at 100 percent, even though he had been diligent about working out during his injury. Every game was a fight to get into the playoffs.

Soon there were only a few games left in the season, and the Predators hadn't secured a playoff spot. But after the final regular-season game was played on April 9, the Predators had snuck into the playoffs with 94 points, securing the last wild card slot in the Western Conference. They were still in the game! P.K. had played in 66 of the 82 regular-season games, scoring 10 goals and earning 30 helpers for 40 points — and every single point had mattered. Nashville fans were ecstatic to see their team, and P.K. Subban, go to playoff action!

While the fans got their jerseys ready for the playoffs — many now had Subban on the back! — P.K. and the Predators got focused on the ice *and* in the dressing room. The team was really gelling, and P.K. talked about how much he loved his new teammates. He had totally embraced being a Predator. Of course, a chance at the Cup was exciting as well. Since the Canadiens were out of playoff action, his fans in Montreal cheered him on, too! He got tweets of support and photos from his young fans at the Montreal Children's Hospital. P.K. was humbled and determined to make them proud.

The Nashville Predators were to face the Chicago Blackhawks in the first round. The Blackhawks had come first in the Western Conference with 109 points. Plus, in the five games the two teams had played during the regular season, the Blackhawks had won four. P.K. knew this was not going to be an easy series.

WHAT DOES P.K. DO IN THE OFF-SEASON?

TRAIN! HIS REGIMEN INCLUDES WEIGHTLIFTING, SPRINTS, HURDLES AND LOTS OF STRETCHING.

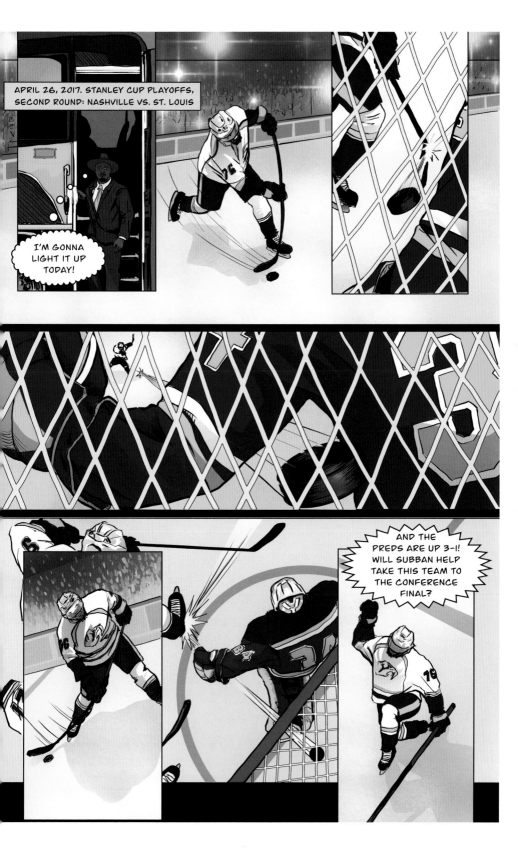

SO CLOSE . . .

The Nashville Predators were off to the Stanley Cup Final, just like P.K. had predicted! The series was against Sidney Crosby and the Pittsburgh Penguins. The Predators were hyped and so were the fans in Nashville. This team was making history for the franchise and P.K. had played a big part in it. It was the first time the Predators had made it to the Stanley Cup Final since they entered the NHL in 1998.

The series started in Pittsburgh. Although the Penguins only managed to get 12 shots on net during the entire first game, they still won 5–3. This was a tough loss for the Predators because they had made 26 shots. P.K. worked hard on the blue line and was solid with his hits. He was especially relentless on Sidney Crosby, their captain. Crosby knew how to win the Cup; he had to be stopped. The second game was much like the first. Nashville came out blasting, ending up with 38 shots on net compared to the Penguins' 29, but they still lost 4–1.

Down by two games, the Predators went home to their fans. The Predators came out flying in front of the hometown crowd, but after the first period they were down by a goal. They regrouped in the dressing room. Then the Predators started scoring!

The Penguins got frustrated and really physical . . . and P.K. seemed to be in the middle of all the battles. P.K. was, again, working hard to make sure Crosby was getting zero shots on net. Tensions were high and Crosby even ended up taking a boarding penalty. At the end of the second period, the score was 3–1 for the Predators. After the final whistle, the Predators had won 5–1! P.K. and Crosby exchanged words as they left the ice, raising a few eyebrows.

The fourth game was also in Nashville and P.K. pestered Crosby the entire time. Finally Sidney got so frustrated he got on top of P.K. and tried to push his head into the ice. But Nashville still won the game 4–1. They'd tied the series at 2–2!

Pittsburgh won the fifth game 6–0. Nashville's best chance in the sixth game came with 6:41 remaining in the third period. P.K. passed to his teammate Colton Sissons in the slot, but Sissons' snap shot bounced off the right post. Nashville lost the game 2–0, and the Penguins won the Cup in back-to-back shutouts.

Although the Predators ultimately lost, it was a roller-coaster ride of a Stanley Cup Final. The fans were very proud of their team — and their new hotshot defenceman.

P.K. KEEPS ON ROLLING

In the 2017–18 season, P.K.'s second with Nashville, he played in all 82 games, finishing with 16 goals and 43 assists for 59 points. But no game was like the one on December 8, 2017. The Predators were playing the brand-new Vegas Golden Knights — who had P.K.'s little brother Malcolm in goal! This was the 10th time in NHL history that a skater faced his brother in net. P.K. thought that playing against Malcolm might have some challenges. "I haven't shot on him in a while," he said before the game, "but I'll find a way." But P.K. didn't find a way. Malcolm made 41 saves, including one against P.K.!

P.K. TAKES A SELFIE WITH HIS FATHER AND BROTHER MALCOLM, WHO WAS A FIRST-ROUND NHL DRAFT PICK IN 2012.

In his off-ice time, P.K. was winning hearts in Nashville, just as he had in Montreal. In October of 2017, he established the Blueline Buddies children's program in Nashville. P.K. wanted to bring police and underprivileged youth together for a meal, some hockey and even autographs and photos with famous players. In December, P.K. had makeup artists give him an aged face and grey beard, and hit the streets disguised as "Eddie," a senior citizen. He handed out candy canes and presents to strangers, and then went on to give a home makeover surprise to one of his Blueline Buddies families. The videos went viral.

P.K.'s generosity was now legendary both in the United States and in Canada, where earlier in the year he received an award from Canada's Governor General David Johnson in honour of his charitable work. He presented P.K. with the Meritorious Service Decoration, for "exceptional deeds that bring honour to Canada."

WHAT IS P.K.'S NOT-SO-SECRET SUPERPOWER?

DANCING! HE OUT-FLOSSED HIS COMPETITORS AT THE 2018 NICKELODEON KIDS' CHOICE AWARDS.

ANOTHER RUN FOR THE CUP

At the end of the season, the Predators were off to the playoffs again. More than that, the Predators had definitely improved during the regular season. They won the 2018 NHL President's Trophy for best regular-season record, with 117 points. Sports pundits were predicting that they would go all the way and win the Stanley Cup.

Their first matchup was against the Colorado Avalanche. In that series, P.K. was a huge contributor on the power play. Whenever he got on the ice, he stopped scoring chances. P.K. also picked up two assists in the second game, and another in the sixth and final game. The Predators won the series 4–2.

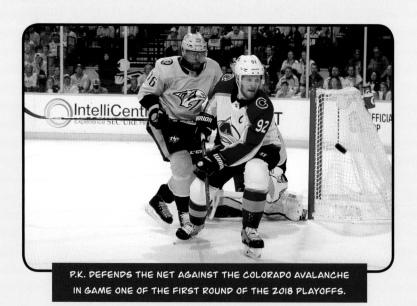

P.K. DEFENDS THE NET AGAINST THE COLORADO AVALANCHE IN GAME ONE OF THE FIRST ROUND OF THE 2018 PLAYOFFS.

Next they played the Winnipeg Jets. This series played out like a ping-pong game. Winnipeg won the first game 4–1, but Nashville responded and won the second game 5–4, with P.K. earning a goal and an assist. Winnipeg won the third game 7–4 but Nashville came right back again and won game four 2–1. This was a big game for P.K. because he scored Nashville's winning goal! With the series tied at two games each, Winnipeg won the next game 6–2. Nashville refused to give up and won the sixth game 4–0. It was down to the seventh and final game. P.K. scored the lone goal for Nashville, but Winnipeg ultimately won it 5–1. This was the end of the season for the Predators.

Even though his Stanley Cup dreams ended early once again, P.K. had had such a good season that for the second time in his career he was nominated for the Norris Trophy for best defenceman. The other nominees were Victor Hedman from the Tampa Bay Lightning and Drew Doughty — P.K.'s former World Junior teammate — from the Los Angeles Kings. P.K. didn't win this time but he did get a different kind of honour that summer. P.K. was chosen as the cover athlete for the *NHL 19* video game. He was ecstatic because this was one of his favourite games!

TRUE GREATNESS

On the ice, P.K. is one of the NHL's best defencemen. Off it, he stands up for what he thinks is right. When P.K. heard that a young hockey player was receiving racist taunts, he sent the 13-year-old a video message. P.K. said, "You gotta believe in yourself and don't let nobody tell you what you can and can't do."

No matter what P.K. does — playing hockey, dealing with the media, having fun with family and friends or helping others — he does it with talent, positivity, honesty and passion. P.K. Subban has always been a standout; now he's a role model, too.

BEHIND THE SCENES OF THE 2016 NHL WINTER CLASSIC, P.K. AND HOCKEY LEGEND WILLIE O'REE MEET A YOUNG FAN.